Dolphins Don't Run Marathons

26.2 loving thoughts on why you
should not run a marathon.

Sam Brand

Sam Brand

Illustrated by Daniel Lichter.
All rights reserved.

First published 2015

This hardcover edition was published in 2015

Contents

To my dear family, who have given me so much inspiration and encouragement which allowed me to give up the long runs and become a dolphin.

Mile 1: *The animal marathon world.*

There are basically three kinds of human animals in the marathon running jungle - the human ant, the human chimp and the human dolphin.

The human ant is simply a marathon runner ,running long steady runs, with a small head and big eyes.

Always running, looking tired and sad, rarely smiling, with all kinds of personality disorders. They always seem to worry about their health, and they tend to live a stressful life. They love to approach pain and avoid pleasure.

Human ant runners are in a constant battle with themselves. It's hard for ants to change; they keep doing the same exercise and will invest all their energy in the wrong kinds of runs.

Human ants love to think very highly of themselves, but the perspective of an ant's view is less than an inch from the ground.

Human ants always think they know best. I myself was a human ant for many years, so trust me: I was wrong. Ants are just lost in their colony.

The human chimpanzee is one of those people who don't like sports.

They may do some exercise from time to time, sure - but it's not an integral part of their everyday lives.

They will always choose a social activity that makes them feel good, like going out for coffee with a friend over going to the gym.

They are your family members, friends or colleagues at work. Basically, they are all those people around you who are not simply running, running and running.

In my ant years, I used to think that human chimps were a bunch of lazy guys who missed it all completely. I used to think they didn't have the discipline or endurance that it takes to be a human ant.

It took me a while to understand that the human chimps are much more intelligent than the human ants and, it's scientifically proven, they are much happier than human ants as well.

Human chimps are able to be happy for others without being jealous. They will tell you how amazing you are for running those long runs simply to be supportive and nice.

Human ants are just entertainment for the human chimps.

The human dolphin is an active, athletic type of person who manages to achieve a balance between doing all sorts of sports. And, yes, sex is also included. Lots of sex. The human dolphin enjoys life for what it is.

Human dolphins are cute and happy and have good relationship values. They are wise, have a good social network, and they know what they are doing. They will find ways to incorporate their activities into their lives - not the other way around.

The human dolphins are imaginative, creative and always willing to try all sorts of sports.

The ultimate goal of the human dolphin is happiness and well-being, and the way to achieve this is through being a well-balanced person.

The human dolphin enjoys swimming, yoga, bicycling, golf, sup (Stand Up Paddle surfing), kayaking and many other sports.

Mile 2: *Face the problem instead of facing the "wall"*

My younger brother is the one who got me into running the marathon. He had done a few marathons before and pushed me to do one myself. He knew everything I needed to know to reach the finish line.

I was an ageing human ant, but he always told me "If you can dream it, you can do it."

He is a natural runner. Me? I had to work hard to be one of those serious running human ants; to earn a place among the elite force of the human ants.

Nobody was born to run 26.2 miles. You need to be a human ant. Your body gradually becomes a human ant running machine.

Every beginner human ant knows: just keep on running. Each part of the run becomes part of the story - the marathon story. Every human ant has its own story and each and every human ant will have a conclusion in the end as the story ends one day.

Eventually, most human ant runners will stop running marathons. This will happen because a marathon, in a way, is only a cover story. Human ant runners are only running to escape from something. They are looking for an escape. The running escape.

Human ant runners can't face the real problem. They prefer to face the "wall," but one day all human ant runners will need to search for their own way out so they do not crash and hit the wall of life.

Running a marathon is incredibly time consuming – it's pure work, and work needs to be taken seriously. Human ant runners always have lots of homework to do!

Human ants have to work hard! Their work controls their eating habits, sleeping habits and their personal lives because they take their work home with them. No kidding! This is not a joke, in fact, human ants don't know any jokes but there are plenty of funny ant jokes out there!

They look to get the medal, just as I needed one of my own. That's why, in 2007, I arrived in New York City to run my first marathon - my first human ant marathon. I wish I'd had a wise human dolphin friend back then who would have pulled me away from the wall and led me to the door: the door to the dolphin way of life.

Mile 3: *Get your priorities straight. Happiness comes from the heart, not from the feet. Be there for the ones you love.*

The New York Marathon is reknowned as the most prestigious marathon in the world. The course takes runners through the five boroughs in a beautiful route and it brings together human ant runners from all over the world.

Every serious human ant runner thinks of doing a marathon at least once in their lifetime, the idea of the experience seems memorable and unique to them. Every year, massive numbers of human ants apply to run the New York marathon but only a limited number of human ants are accepted.

To finish a marathon, you must be ready.

Dear human ants: the marathon is vitally important. You must take it seriously. After all, you have worked very hard and have spent a lot of time on it. That is why human ants need to miss important events because they need to keep on practicing the long runs no matter what.

Human ant runners: listen to the wise dolphin and don't miss out on family friendly events just because you need to run after runners.

Mile 4: *There is more to life than one adventure. Look for more supplements of life.*

The difference between humans and animals is that humans aren't born with the endurance for a 26.2 mile run. For humans, there is a high energy cost of running when there really isn't any real need to run long distances when you can walk, hike, golf, climb, swim or kayak.

The benefits of low level aerobic work like walking, hiking, cycling, swimming or kayaking is that it increases the capillary network, increases muscle mitochondria, increases production of fat-burning and fat–transporting enzymes and, finally, it's fun because you can talk with a partner while doing it. High levels of aerobics, on the other hand, require large amounts of dietary carbohydrates (sugar), increase the stress hormone cortisol, increase systemic inflammation, and increase oxidative damage. Over-training causes difficulty in sleeping and persistent fatigue. Between you and me: running for hours is just a boring pain in the ass.

Me? I had to know everything regarding those long runs including the nutrition facts. After reading all about minerals, vitamins and foods, in general, I found myself taking all kinds of pills, powders and gels. I was always looking for the next best sport supplement. My friends and family, those human chimps and dolphins and other ant runners, looked up to me as someone who knew it all and were always asking about my new health trends. I had to maintain professionalism, as a serious human ant should. I found myself in a world of antioxidants, gluten-free diets, Omega 3s and other dietary supplements. In terms of food, I had become a human health fanatic ant.

Human ant runners: supplements may be good for you, but look for the real supplements of life instead of supplements for life.

Mile 5: *Food goes well with happiness. Stop exhausting yourselves searching for perfection in every meal. Life tastes better.*

Searching for the best nutrition caused my list of dos and don'ts to change on a monthly basis, all in the search of the best running nutrition formula for the human ant runners.

The amazing thing was, no matter how many times I had proven myself wrong, no matter how many times I had completely changed my diet I remained trapped in the classic human ant way of life continuing to search for the ultimate nutrition for runners.

I didn't understand how human chimps and dolphins could enjoy a good meal with a good bottle of wine, and good dessert, while I was busy perfecting the marathon meal plan. I didn't understand that these small treats the human dolphins and human chimps shared were, in many ways, helping to create for them better health than any diet could.

Any human dolphin or chimp will tell you that enjoying food is good for you. Runner ants can't enjoy food because they have "food guilt." So, human dolphins and chimps readers: please show your human ant friends the way.

Human ants go for chocolate from time to time. It's good for the heart, and it gives you energy as well. Cocoa contains antioxidants that increase blood flow and trigger natural endorphins. And because the increased blood flow to your body will also increase blood flow to the brain, cocoa will actually make you smarter and help improve your memory. You may become a super smart human dolphin one day.

Human dolphins are so smart. They are able to improve themselves by doing things they love and enjoy. Human ants, you can do that, too. Let those wise human dolphins show you the way! Start 'eating' positive opportunities or ultimately, you will starve to death.

Mile 6: *First thing you'll need to do, in order to be the life of the party, is to join the party.*

Most of the human ant runners spent the day before the race doing everything in their power to prepare themselves for the race. Resting after lunch, doing short runs, stretching a lot, visualizing the course of the run, staying relaxed, staying hydrated and going to sleep early.

Me? I had to follow the group. My group was made up of my wife, my brothers and their wives. All of these people were chimps and dolphins who came to New York to support me. They were there for me. But the truth was, they were really there for themselves. Activities and celebrations started with breakfast and continued through lunch, and dinner. They came to New York to enjoy it so I guess it's only fair, isn't it?

It was their world against mine.

I asked them to try to go out early, but dinner started at 10pm that night. We entered a trendy restaurant uptown. We were a party of eight, headed towards the bar for a drink, raising our glasses and toasting the human dolphin in celebration of his birthday. We were one big happy group

23:30 PM Our table was full of food and alcohol. There were lots of jokes about runners – many of them about me. At one point, one of the gang, a human dolphin, a bit drunk, said, "Skip the marathon! I will get you a medal." I went mad. Real human mad ant. I reminded myself once again that they were all there to support me and it was the human dolphin's birthday we were celebrating that night, so I just tried to keep calm. They all seemed so cheerful, wild with all the endorphins, happy in the big city, and I was deep in my human ant world, nervous and aggravated.

It was clear that they were a happy group of human chimps and dolphins.

00:00 AM They were still a lively bunch. Arguing about where the following day's feasts would be. I looked at my watch, thinking of tomorrow's run -the pace, the distance, the heart rate, the elevation. There was the 2007 New York Marathon waiting for me…

01:00 AM The party was still going. I couldn't help myself anymore so I reminded them that the run was in the morning. I was going to have to get up early, run from the hotel towards the library on 42nd street, and then take the bus to Staten Island. But the gang was thinking about dinner party desserts.

02:00 AM Dinner was finally over. We grabbed our coats and headed out of the restaurant and, still, the human chimps and dolphins were joking around.

02:30 AM We arrived at the hotel. I was trying my best to fall asleep, but I couldn't. My lovely wife, a happy, good looking human chimp, was looking for sex with her husband ant the night before the marathon. I had heard the myth that sex the night before running a marathon is not recommended. I explained to her the importance of a runner's sleep. She fell asleep a few minutes later.

I was totally nervous about my marathon and couldn't fall asleep. I wanted to be a different animal. I wanted to be a dolphin. I was looking for help.

Mile 7: *The only long road worth running a marathon on is the road to happiness in life.*

Getting ready on the morning of a marathon is a ceremony all on its own.

I got on the bus on my way to the starting point. All the other human ant runners on the bus seemed very serious. There was a lot of tension in the air. We crossed the big double decker bridge into Staten Island. There were so many busses, one right after the other. The colony ant busses were enroute. Finally we got off. All the human ants got off the busses.

The sight was overwhelming. It seemed like a real live human ant farm. The number of human ant runners was unbelievable. There was a worship service tent for the religious ants, a stretching area, and all kinds of areas supporting us human ant runners.

I looked up and saw nothing but blue sky. It was a bit chilly that day. The whole area was packed with tight security; we were very secure human ant runners. Besides an enormous number of policemen, I noticed police sharp shooters, helicopters and jets flying overhead.

There were so many human ant runners out there, dressed in all kinds of outfits. And, there were so many American flags and flags from different countries but, let's face it, we were all human ants with one goal. We all wanted to win a marathon.

All together but alone. Brothers in arms but conquering the long run alone.

There were human ants running dressed as the Statue of Liberty, basketball players, Mickey Mouse, Minnie Mouse and in other crazy outfits.

I got distracted by the announcer who said, "God bless all of you, God bless your marathon, God bless America..."

I was thinking to myself: "God bless all the human ant runners. God bless the colony."

We were asked to get closer to the chutes. We started walking up to the bridge, both the top and bottom of the bridge were full of human ants - the bridge of ants. The wise human dolphin could teach the human ants how to build a bridge to happiness.

Mile 8: *You better pace yourself before you kill yourself.*

First mile-The Verrazano Bridge

You can hardly call it running. There are so many human ant runners that it's like a big traffic jam. You walk or jog at best. As the path opens up a bit and we actually start running at a comfortable pace, I couldn't help but think that I had never seen so many human ant runners with their backs to me. There were close to two million fans out there, all excited as if they were about to run themselves - but that's human chimps for you. Happy, positive and loud.

8th mile - Brooklyn The

day of the marathon was a day of pure love between the human ants and human chimpanzees. Human chimps are your biggest fans for one day. They want you to do it; they want to see you do well. It's a New York City holiday. Human chimps formed bands and sang songs. Volunteer human chimps handed out bananas; there were human chimp reporters, and medical human chimps. There were funny human chimps with inspirational signs to make you laugh. All of them were cheering. What was it about these human chimpanzees that made me feel good that day?

The pain was there during the run, but these human chimps would not let you give up. Maybe they know something the human ant runners don't know. The human chimps don't give a damn about "the wall." Human chimps never even heard of it. They were all cheering the 50,000 human ant runners. But it felt as though they were only cheering for me.

13th mile - Queens

The optimistic human ant runner will tell you that the glass is half full when crossing the 13th mile. The pessimistic human ant runner will tell you that there are still 13 miles to go. They are both simple, foolish ants. Trust the human dolphins: they enjoy whatever they are doing and don't even bother wondering whether the glass is half full or half empty. They know how to be happy. Ant runners don't. Human dolphins always find the answers to all the questions the human ant runners seek.

16th mile - Manhattan

There were some unbelievable human ant runners out there, like an 80 year old human ant running with a trainer, a blind human ant runner, and a female human ant running with one leg.

21st Mile - Bronx Ant runners are most likely to hit "the wall" around the Bronx.

26.2th mile Crossing the finish line in Central Park is when I completed my first New York City human ant marathon.

Human ant runners out there: once you have completed the marathon, you may find yourself sinking into a world of emptiness. Listen to the wise dolphin and make it your lucky day. It's your short term decision making day. Move on to the new sporting life of the dolphin - the human dolphin's magic life.

Mile 9: *The view is always better from the sidelines.*
That way you are looking in all directions.

Central Park is a New York landmark. Symbolically, it's where the New York marathon ends for ant runners and life begins for human chimps and human dolphins. Central Park is the golden ground for human ants, human chimps and human dolphins.

The park, stretching over 843 acres, offers so many different activities and options. From eating a sandwich under a tree and enjoying nature in the middle of the city, to taking your children to the zoo, rollerblading, running and so much more. It's a perfect place, full of life and, oh, so beautiful.

Human ant runners can stand and see the park from different aspects, but they never choose to. They fail to see it as an opportunity for transition - the bridge to a new world.

The horse carriage ride in Central Park is so romantic for human chimps and human dolphins. For the human ant runners, it's just a ride.

For me, as I transformed from a human ant to a human dolphin, I was able to see the Park change before my very eyes. The zoo in the Park gave me the drive to see the animal world as it related to the long running marathon world. I learned, if you look hard enough, all the answers, to the most complicated questions, are right there in the Park.

Today, when I go there, I see life. I am not sure human ant runners see it all. The wise human dolphin says they see only the Central Park running trails.

This place did make the change for me. It became a whole new world of symbols which enabled me to change the way I see reality around me. I now enjoy the small bridges in the Park - they are the bridges to a whole new world out there.

Human ant runners from all over the world, do yourselves a favor, next time you are in New York, when you finish the race, spend some time enjoying the Park. Sit and think. It will be your gateway back to being a happy human dolphin.

The green trees in the Park will give you some inspiration to think about change. Some of the trees are 50-foot high, if you haven't noticed. Unfortunately, human ant runners never look up when they run.

Just walking in the Park will make you a better person. When you walk in the Park, you begin to imagine. It isn't a coincidence that a permanent "Imagine" memorial to John Lennon is situated right there on the west side of the park and the landscape around it is named after another Beatles song, "Strawberry Fields Forever."

Human ant runners, make sure you enjoy the Park next time you're out there. Don't just run through it. Look deep into the human dolphin's eyes and imagine how the human dolphin is perceiving the world.

Mile 10: *Exercising alone only improves your body. Exercising with the ones you love improves both the body and the bonds between you.*

No matter how old you are, there is a lot you can do in Central Park. There is something for everybody.

Try riding in the park. Thousands of bike riders enjoy the Park every day. Human chimps, wearing helmets, roller-skating in the park and human dolphins on bicycles riding for fun.

During every visit to the Park you will encounter people rollerblading, dancing and doing gymnastics, practicing yoga, playing and walking with a loved one, or visiting the baseball fields. Human dolphins and human chimps go there to play and have fun. There is even a theater in the Park. You won't be bored human ants, you only need to look around you.

Ant runners, as the wise human dolphin says: "you are the actors, in a one day show, in the Park the day of the marathon, but on the other 364 days of the year you simply don't exist."

Whenever I reach the carousel in the Park, I stop to watch. I see it turning and turning, reaching nowhere. I think back to the days of me being a human ant runner. I used to run in circles, going nowhere.

Now, walking in the Park, I see Central Park as much more than just a finish line in the New York City marathon.

Today, in every visit, I make sure I spend a lot of time in Central Park, giving it the utmost respect. It is a wonderful place. Human ant runners, open your eyes. Next time you run in the park, look at your surroundings with the eyes of a dolphin. Enjoy it with the people you love.

Mile 11: *Read all about it.*

The New York Times has a nice, special section for human ant runners the day after the marathon. So, after waking up in the early morning, the day after the marathon, the first thing a human ant will do is buy the paper. Today: they are the news.

Human chimps and human dolphins will read all the other sections. But you … you are in there. Your name and your running time in a special "finisher results" section with results up to 4:54 hours.

All I knew was I had to finish under 4:54 hours. Otherwise, I would not be in the news. I was a fast human ant runner. I made the news.

Mile 12: *Don't throw your life into the wastepaper basket. Be a part of the action.*

My human dolphin and human chimp friends invited me to join them to watch a basketball game in Madison Square Garden. In the past when this happened, I always said no. What runner ant had time for these things? But on this occasion, due to a sharp aching pain in my right leg that prevented me from running, I had nothing else to do. I thought to myself: "This is a good chance to see their world. I can see the guys and I get a chance to pretend I'm an easygoing person."

It was the opening night. The atmosphere was incredible. The arena was full of human chimps and dolphins enjoying the game. Fans cheering out loud, laughing, eating popcorn and drinking beer. There were no human ant runners anywhere in sight. Just a few days prior, I was one of 50,000 identical human ants on a mission. Part of a big colony mission. Here, I was very different.

My chimp and dolphin friends were already having their second hot dog. I was thinking: "What are they doing?!" The amount of beer was crazy, and the food was extremely processed! But, I decided I was going to be part of the gang. After all, it's not like I eat like this every day and, I convinced myself, it's a part of the experience.

I reached for some fries. Both my friends looked at me surprised, as they knew I usually only ate healthy foods and they'd heard all my lectures about nutrition.

I ate those fries and they sure went great with the beer. "Welcome to the gang." It wasn't easy letting go, but I tried my best that night. I wanted to be one of them. I hadn't enjoyed myself this much in a long time, and that was healthy in and of itself.

After the game, I was the one driving. You can always count on the reliable human ant to avoid losing control and drinking too much. We were chatting about the game. The human dolphin in the back said, "The best part was you having that beer!" we all laughed. "Listen Ant," he said, "Next Thursday is bowling night. You have to come."

"Think it over, we want you to be there. You'll have fun." The human dolphin asked me to meet the next evening for a drink at the bar. Is happiness just around the corner?

Mile 13: *A little advice from a big dolphin. If you ever take advice, take it from a human dolphin.*

Dolphins are not considered one of the smartest in the animal kingdom for nothing. I actually heard that dolphins have large brains in comparison to their body size and that they can communicate a large range of emotions like sadness, happiness and excitement to their group and in turn they interact by helping each other, playing together and enjoying one another's touch and company. What an amazing, adjustable creature. Even baby dolphins can swim the moment they are born, which is more than you can say for chimps, ants, and humans. The dolphin lives in perfect harmony with its surroundings. My human dolphin friend was no different. A true, wise human dolphin.

We met around 8:00pm. Human ant runners never really get time to know their true friends until they get injured.

We ordered drinks and started talking. My human dolphin friend seemed to be a very special dolphin.

Whenever we met, I felt completely inspired by his wisdom and wished I was a bit more like him. I wish I was born a dolphin.

We talked about the marathon for a few minutes. My dolphin friend seemed impressed but quickly changed the subject by asking me about my beautiful human chimp wife and my human dolphin kids, then he updated me on his family. He took out his wallet and showed me pictures. Wow, his children certainly had grown up since I last saw them.

"Listen Ant," he said, noticing my discomfort. "I don't have anything against running, so don't get me wrong, but, don't be tempted by that crazy mileage log. It's nice and everything, but go search for other temptations every once in a while. I feel like you're missing quite a lot of what's really important. Sometimes we need to change or our future will be exactly like our past ... only with lots of injuries."

I wanted to let him know how running was good for your body, and your soul. How it gives you a sense of achievement and how fulfilling it is, but I didn't. I had my doubts.

"Your soul needs more than running up and down the streets. Concentrate and learn new things every day instead of doing the same thing you did the day before and the day before that, and the day before that. Human ant runners, you don't want to end up a boring old human ant that only talks about the running days before you get injured. People live longer and longer these days you know… by 2050, there will be more people over 65 than under five. Think about your sporting future life after the marathons."

Mile 14: *You are not a just single wave but a small part of a big ocean.*

I owe my human dolphin friend for my new sporting life. I am now a part of a big ocean.

My friend, the wise human dolphin taught me one last lesson that day: I am a part of something bigger than me, whether I like it or not. Just like a wave is a part of an ocean, I need to search for the bond in sports with my family and friends.

Ant runners, even in the hardest moments of your life, take a look at yourself in the mirror and look for the smiley, singing, happy dolphin looking back at you. He is there.

Thank you Mr. Dolphin. I am now having fun, I'm involved in sports, and spending more time with friends and family.

Mile 15: *Try new things the dolphin way. Stop being such a pain in the ant. Go for the mental exercise as well. Release tension and increase your body's awareness.*

On the flight back home from the New York City Marathon, I could hardly move; I was trying to stretch all the time, and I was looking for the most comfortable position. I spent the entire flight thinking about my future in the running world.

I thought about my New York human dolphin friend, and about the time I spent training for the marathon. I realized I spent a lot of time with myself, but I had a lot of memories. It's hard to share these memories with family. They could never understand the experience, but at least I could show them the medal. The New York Marathon medal. I certainly worked hard for it, running for over four hours.

Family and friends were expecting me to keep talking about the marathon and they were surprised when I changed the subject. After all that time in my own world, in my own colony, I wanted to be one of them.

Here is a word of advice about those first few weeks trying to "leave the colony", don't take it hard if friends don't ask you to join them for a match of tennis, a hiking trip, kayaking, or any other activity; you always said "No" in the past, didn't you? In the past, you were only concerned with training for the marathon. It's exactly like coming back from capture. Years have passed and now people need to get to know you again.

Even my beautiful, happy human chimp wife had to get used to this new sporting life. Suddenly I didn't disappear to run on the weekends, I was there instead.

I personally know of a lot of relationships that suffered greatly from the long distance running lifestyle. A few even ended in divorce, and I have heard of many others. The first days without the long runs are hard. You have to force yourself to stay in bed longer, not leave before the sunrise. It gets really hard when your wife turns to you and says, "Do you want to join me today for a yoga class?"

The thing about human ant runners, especially serious ones, is that all they know is running. They don't do things like yoga. If they were tried to be forced, they would hide under their mattresses.

Me? Taking a yoga class? Is that real? I didn't even know if they would let me in. I was so ashamed to be seen there… the only comfort was that no human ant I knew was going to be there. Most of the class was made up of human chimps and, maybe, a few human dolphins.

It took 90 minutes for me to realize I was wrong. So wrong… Yoga is more than a breathing exercise; it's a means to finding your path to your own true self.

It improves your strength, balance, flexibility, and peace of mind. Human ants don't have any peace of mind as ants are always in battle with themselves. Yoga is a guaranteed way to help you become a human dolphin.

Even if you are not yet convinced about leaving your colony, take-off just for a while. Say you have something important to do and practice some yoga. Yoga will make you ant runners feel better, more relaxed, and your immune system will get stronger. Your back pain will start to disappear. Yoga lowers the resting heart rate, increases endurance, and improves the maximum intake of oxygen during exercise.

Human ants: yoga lowers your cortisol levels and it has been found to lower blood sugar levels as well; it can even make you grow taller. You will also have shorter recovery times after races, and the benefits are not only physical.

Yoga relieves you from the hectic pace of modern life. For you depressed human ants, it would only do you good. You think you know your body well, but you'd be surprised how much yoga can teach you about your body. Greater ant body awareness.

So human ants, try to make the change. Go find which yoga is good for you. Get your peace of mind. Improve your breathing. Stop being anti-yoga and join your first class. Yoga for the ant beginners. Get inspired. Start to catch your breath!

Human ants, yoga will help you achieve a sense of balance, relaxation, and well-being.

Mile 16: *Go for short runs and long sex mileage.*

For human ant runners, GPS stands for Ground, Pace and Speed. That's what they care about. Pace, pace, pace. Speed, speed, speed. They love statistics; they love data. They love knowing the data and statistics of everything so they can fight the stats. As for the human dolphins and chimps, GPS stands for Games, Pleasure and lots of Sex.

They love games as it is time spent in good spirits and with loved ones. A game is an activity that involves being happy. Pleasure is another key ingredient in their lives. Time with friends, and going out with them. Sex is no different. After all, most animals have sex for the purpose of reproduction, but dolphins are like humans and have sex sometimes only for pleasure. Human dolphins love to have lots of sex. Human ant runners don't. They are always too tired.

For human dolphins and human chimps, sex is a good interval workout. It brings the heart rate to higher levels. They wish to keep it at a high level for a long period. But God created intervals to be short. Both human dolphins and human chimps prefer to enjoy quality time in the bedroom rather than running the long run.

Human ant runners, don't blame yourselves. You are exhausted from all the long runs; you wake up at crazy hours when it's still dark outside.

Take it easy when it comes to romance. Your partners are not used to your running pace nor should they be. It's only you who look to finish the course. You want to control your lovemaking like you control your long running sessions, but there is no need to be a control freak ant.

Human ant runners, stop thinking of how long it takes to get to the finish line when it's comes to sex.

Human ants, it's better to slow down from time to time. Roads are for cars. Actually, try using a car. You may find yourself having wild sex with your partner in the car. Trust the dolphins; they know best. Sex is for pleasure and it's not as good if you're exhausted or woke up three hours before everyone else. Learn from the human dolphins who enjoy life and let others enjoy it as well. The human ant runners need some lessons from the human dolphins on how to be romantic. Sex by itself is a bond. Make it a strong bond. The dolphin sex bond.

Human ant runners, listen to the wise dolphin. Shorter runs will do you good. Exercise overload will wear you out. Dolphins conserve energy for better sex. It is a workout activity, after all.

Mile 17: *The world isn't flat. Make sure you use all of it.*
Ants: you will love getting wet.

It's hard for human ants to stop running. It's even harder to start swimming, but human ants, trust me, there is something amazing about being in the water. Any sort of water sport. It can be a pool, a lake or an ocean.

After I quit the long runs, I started to enjoy water sports.

Dear human ant runners, I urge you to try it. Don't pretend to be tough. There is a new world out there and it's wet and wonderful. It's magic. The wise human dolphin knew this all along.

Try to imagine the human dolphin successfully convincing the human ant to join him for a ride in a kayak. Going out into an open sea with waves that can't be controlled, with winds that can't be controlled then paddling out a few miles.

Watching the kayaks from the beach, I started to convince myself it was a fun sport. So, I rented myself a sea kayak and pulled it towards the water. It was my first time so, naturally, I was afraid. I wore my dolphin suit. I was going in.

Handling the first few small waves was easier than I had expected. Next thing I knew I was in deep water. I kept thinking that ants don't know how to swim. Ants drown in water. To my surprise, the wind didn't seem to bother me and the view was beautiful. Kayaking turned out to be an adventure; a gateway to nature. Starting in the morning on the golden sandy beach, I had to adapt to something else: Self-reliance. Paddling for two hours in the sea is not an easy job, but slowly I did start to understand the secrets of the waves. I started to love it.

I felt the dolphin in me. I was enjoying myself in a way I never had before. As a dolphin, I started to feel the freedom and started enjoying the sup (Stand Up Paddle surfing) as well as the ocean. My connection to the water felt so good. After all, 70 percent of the earth's surface is water. Being a human dolphin on a sup (Stand Up Paddle surfing), makes a lot of sense. It is a huge playground. Use it. There are many dolphins with sups out there. It's a great water sport as well. Human ant runners, listen to the wise dolphin and challenge yourselves with water sports.

Mile 18: *Runner's ant face and dead ant butt.*

Admit it human ant runners; look in the mirror. The only thing you see during the runs are those falling runners' faces and the dead butts of the human ants in front of you.

In the pool, you don't see human ants. The human dolphins start their day in the water like it is some kind of meditation. What a way to start your day... just hearing the water makes you calm.

Just like with yoga, I got into swimming with an angry attitude. Mad. What the hell am I doing here with these lazy swimmers? I didn't understand them at all.

I saw some human dolphin swimmers at one corner of the pool and I saw some human dolphins in the deep water doing water aerobics. I asked to join them. Human ants, trust me, dolphins know what they are doing.

With water aerobics in the deep end of the pool, you have to move your full body quite rapidly as to keep your head above water; it is a full body workout. I couldn't believe how hard it was.

One of the guys could see that I was struggling. He looked at me and said, "Think positive thoughts. Negative thoughts will only make you drown." I was amazed to find that he was right. When you swim, you talk to yourself positively. Water aerobics is so hard that you just can't afford the weight of negativity.

Ants, water aerobics works on all your muscles. I enjoyed it a lot and now I am going to go to the pool to do swimming workouts and, from time to time, water aerobics. Water workouts burn a lot of calories. Being in the water is an anti-aging cure in and of itself. The water can get your heart rate up and provide a great workout. The extra resistance of the water makes it ideal for muscles and strengthening workouts. Your body becomes weightless, giving you new challenges. It's also low impact on your joints but high impact on your cardiovascular system.

Human ants out there, go swimming with a smile. Did you see any smiles on runners' faces during the race? Never. Guys, I was looking, and I didn't see anyone out there in the marathon smiling. Actually, the thing you see the most is not even faces; you see the asses of the ants running in front of you.

Did you know that the human ant runners who run those long runs are literally ruining their smiles? Long running can cause more oxygen or free-radical damage, which can break down or damage the skin's supportive fibers. Your cheeks start to sag from all the bouncing and pounding while you run. The end result of all of this is that you get a gaunt, hollow, pre-aged, skeletal look.

Human ant runners, you're doing a lot of unnecessary damage to your whole body.

Besides your face, marathon running puts extraordinary stress on your heart. Long runs are correlated with higher levels of heart problems. The damage that endurance athletes do to their hearts adds up over time and, in this case, more is certainly not better.

30 to 50 percent of runners show increased levels of enzymes that are typically related with heart attacks and heart failures. Human ants, just give your heart a break.

There is the immune system to consider as well, and helping it will help to keep your body healthier for longer. You need your immune system, so support it. Don't stop running; just keep it easy by doing short runs. Make your life an adventure - not work. And do lots of other activities as well.

Another unpleasant result is the Dead Butt Syndrome, which is characterized by severe hip pain during and after running long distances. Train yourself to run shorter runs; walk, bike, swim, hike, kayak, etc, to keep from declining cardiac output, losing lung capacity, losing bone density, losing lean muscle mass, and losing estrogen. At least, 40 to 50 percent of runners experience injuries on an annual basis. Make yourself a master plan so you can stay super fit as you age.

Human ants, look at yourselves. It's just running! And, it's your body that will suffer the consequences of your choice. Help it and watch over it well. One thing I can tell you about the human dolphins, some are exercising, some are playing, some are just floating, but all of them are smiling. Whether the runner's face is myth or reality, face it human ant runners, you have a problem.

Mile 19: *Let your mind run in all directions. My last and final New York City selfie ant marathon.*

I really wanted to see what drives the human ant runners; I tried to find the human ant's focus.

I decided to do one last race as it would help me look at myself up close. I do believe long running is an anti-social activity as you are completely immersed in your own world.

All ant runners talk to themselves, but I needed to see myself from a different angle. I connected my camera to a long wireless rod, then printed on both sides of my shirt the words "Selfie-Run" and went out to conquer the New York City Marathon with a less serious, more reflective point of view. Everyone was looking at me as we got ready to head off. This time everyone was tense but me. I was calm; I am a human dolphin trying to find solutions to all the ant problems in life.

It was the New York City 2009 Marathon, the 40th New York City Marathon. And me? I'm a part of it, as a self-experimenting, running dolphin.

We started the run. I took it easy, running a slow, steady pace. I was feeling sorry for myself and all the ant runners out there who were just starting the "mission." I felt sorry for them because I knew that in their heads they were thinking, "You've practiced for this day and now you can't make mistakes." I wanted to shout out loud and say, "Ant runners! The whole thing is a mistake!"

Running with the rod wasn't easy. It would have been nice to see myself and the other ant runners around; to see what we looked like as the run progressed.

We passed the first mile. Human ant runners were sticking their faces near me so they could be in the picture with me. After another few miles, none of them bothered to make the effort. They were too busy concentrating and were already tired. I was smiling the whole run. I was laughing at myself and at all the unhappy, suffering human ant runners around me as they were all a reflection of my previous self.

I was able to film things the runners don't usually see as human ants have a pretty narrow view. I was filming the crowd, the policemen and the photographers, the kids, myself and others, but the most important thing I was filming was the human dolphins and human chimps out there - part of the happy, cheering crowd.

This run made me realize I had found the outer world through my inner voice which had been telling me I was different from all these other runners. I was proud I was escaping this ant world. This is what winning is all about. I was searching for the truth in this last and final long run. During the whole run I talked to myself about what a mistake it is to be addicted to these long runs. Finally, positive thinking comes when you become a human dolphin - even your inner voice changes, and it feels so much more mature and happy…

When I looked at pictures of the run, I felt proud of not fitting in and, instead, of standing out. Human ant runners, find the power to stop the long runs. It will enable health and happiness. Human ant runners, listen to the wise dolphin. Half marathons and full marathons are done in a matter of hours, but runners spend months training for these 13.1 and 26.2 mile races. Change your lifestyle – change your life. Change how far you run.

Mile 20: *Talking to yourself is great, but why not trying to enjoy talking to others? Human ant runners: shut up about running.*

It has been about a year without the long runs. I have enjoyed a lot of freedom by being away from the running. I feel more connected to everything. Even my body. Now I have time for everything in my life.

It all started with a meeting. Just a standard business lunch my secretary had set up so I could close a deal. "Shouldn't take long", I'm thinking, an hour at the most.

I was 10 minutes late. I excused myself to everyone, blaming it on traffic. "So how have you all been? Did I miss anything important?" I smiled. "A few minutes of small talk," I told myself, "and I'm out of here."

Suddenly, I noticed the rhythm of the conversation was changing. From relaxed small talk into something serious. "This is not good", I'm thinking to myself. Our colleague, a 45 year old, female lawyer started talking about how she had been in the process of running for a few months and she was training to do a half marathon soon. I started getting frustrated as I knew where the conversation was heading but my lawyer, who started running this year, got all excited.

The meeting drove me crazy. It was like being back on a battlefield. None of them had anything else to talk about other than running. My lawyer forgot about the deal; he was representing himself - not me. There went my plan for a quick, successful deal.

I gave in. They both looked at me as a human queen ant as I had been there before them. I did marathons. And, where of all places? In New York City, the world's biggest marathon. Human ant runners, listen to the wise dolphin and quit the long runs. If you can't stop telling the whole world about your long runs, then just shut up and keep on running.

Mile 21: *You are what you breathe. Ants: take a breath of fresh air.*

Human ant runners, listen to the wise human dolphin and stop running on the hot streets. In those long runs, you breathe in polluted air. Heat and pollution together cause greater reductions in lung functionality and running performance. Human ants running on the streets inhale Ozone Carbon Monoxide and Sulfur Dioxide, decreasing blood and oxygen flow to the muscles. Human ant runners, stop running on toxic air.

Human ant runners, you can't run from pollution. It's either you or the drivers who will have to turn off your engines.

Some marathon ant runners already wear masks when they run and, my guess is, the running industry may add a digital tool to measure air pollution to sports watches very soon. And, as well, they should. Ant awareness is growing and there is a new trend for running clean air marathons. Support those clean air runs and stay off the roads as much as possible. Wanna become a dolphin?

Mile 22: *Ants never stop unless they get run over. Better to be a dolphin. Dolphins move on.*

Test yourselves human ant runners. Once you are out of those long runs, never look back. Stay focused.

You are human dolphins now. Run away from those long runs.

Memories of the marathons are nice, but keep them in the past. Leave the marathons as a life memory. Don't test yourself again. This is a turning point in your life.

A while after becoming a happy human dolphin, my lawyer asked me to join him for a running lesson with a new trainer. This could have been a huge mistake, but I was strong.

I am a swimmer now. A real human dolphin. Enjoying kayaking, and sup (Stand Up Paddle surfing), from time to time. I'm through with all of the long runs, but the trainer is trying to bring me back to the ant world. It simply isn't fun anymore.

I was thinking of ways to approach the trainer. I came up with a good idea, I decided I was going to play it "the dumb ant way." "Concentrate on my lawyer, I'm here as a one timer." I tell him. "He is here to improve. To get stronger, faster."

The lawyer was a good ant, he came ready for the lesson, telling the trainer that he wanted to finish half a marathon in under two and a half hours. The lawyer just wanted to run faster. Me? I was confused, not sure of what I was going to say. Ants are never confused. But I was. "I am a dolphin now." Try to tell a guy like the trainer you're not an ant anymore.

After the session, the trainer opened his little notebook, forcing us to make an appointment for the next lesson. I never went back. I love my human dolphin life. The lawyer is still there, a human ant runner, running circles at the stadium, instead of reaching out to find the circle of life.

I am free now. No more ant time. Back to the real, happy world, with a more satisfying life and the big desire to live a dolphin life.

Mile 23: *Human ant's and dolphin's behavior in the animal business world.*

You'd be surprised how much you can tell about a person just by the way he or she exercises. Human ant marathon runner business men and women take a harsh path to their target. Human ants see only the goal they want to reach, they don't care about the means to the end. Even if they hit a wall, the business ant wants the medal no matter what. But sometimes you practice for the marathon and things don't work out as you were planning. You may practice the whole year but Mother Nature has other plans for you that day. Ants can't face failure. They want the winning ticket. But statistics show that some ants just don't make it.

Dolphins always make it. They look at the means to reach their goal as something with a lot of value. They correct things on the way to the road of success. Human ant runners will continue running even if they are hurt. Even if their heart rate is high. Human dolphins will go to a yoga class if they feel it might be good for them, or they take time for swimming, water aerobics, sup (Stand Up Paddle surfing), kayaking and more. Why? Their goal is always the same – being happy.

Human ants love the stress; they enjoy it - but human dolphins don't. They love to see the day coming along. Happy days. Human ants don't understand happiness. Human ants wear all kinds of watches. Dolphins don't wear watches. They have it within them. The sunrise and sunset is the only watch they need.

The human ants need a watch for pace, elevation, and more. Human dolphins enjoy the waves of elevation. They don't fight the hard weather. They don't fight the waves. They never hit a wall. Human ants do.

Human ant runners run in all kinds of weather. They don't care about their immune system. They want the medal. Their body may need rest from time to time but they don't stop. Human dolphins know how to adjust. And that's their biggest advantage when it comes to business.

With respect to the business world, human ants will stick to and hold onto their business plan no matter what. Human dolphins will change their plan from time to time and never look back. They will surround themselves with support. Similar to sports, in business a skilled team with strengths is better than a solo effort.

Countries are the same as people. Some countries handled the world economic crisis well, some collapsed. Ant countries can't cope with changes they must make to their economics. Dolphin countries find it easier. The world is a jungle; the economic world is as well. Human dolphins are quick to learn. Maybe it's the Omega 3 in the dolphin's diet and the fact that they leave time to train their brains as well. It's as important as physical exercise. Twenty minutes of moderate brain exercise improves cognitive functions like memory, creativity, and decision making. The most important muscle to use is the brain. Human ant runners, listen to the wise human dolphin. Even in the economic world, it's important to understand the difference between the short and the long runs.

Mile 24: *Keep it short. Give yourself a head start. Join the short distance runs out there.*

Listen up human ant marathon runners. We the human dolphins and the human chimps thank you for leaving us the leftovers. Those short runs may not seem sexy to you at all, or they may seem like a waste of time. But we love the short runs. They keep us smiling the whole race. Short races are good enough to earn medals, and they have low impact on the body. Go for these refreshing runs.

Human ant runners, go easy on yourselves;
run short distances.

The running world is pushing you to take those long runs for no reason. Trust me ant runners, give yourselves a break and try to run a short race; you can do it with other family members as well. It will keep you on the mental, happy, and social road to being happier with your life.

Human ant runners cannot see people walking in the race. But human dolphins and chimps can walk from time to time. These short races are good enough as they make you feel in shape, happy, and, more important, socially happy. Short social, mental, happy runs. Social runs.

Short is better for longer living.
Human ant runners, listen to the wise human dolphin. All those short runs are packed with lots of health benefits.

Mile 25: *It's a dead end run. Stop running away from yourself.*

Marathons may be considered a symbol of good health and fitness these days as it is a growing worldwide trend.

Human ant marathon runners, bear in mind that the first man ever to run a marathon collapsed and died right after - and you are all following in his footsteps. Running towards a dead end. Does it have to be this way? Stop while you can. Don't run yourself to death. Look for the short and the fun runs.

Happy human chimps and human dolphins around you are likely to help you find the way. Human ant runners, listen to the wise human dolphin and stop being a case study in the runner's world

Mile 26.2: *Human ant runners: listen to the wise human dolphin and BE A DOLPHIN. ALL OTHER ANIMALS ARE ALREADY TAKEN.*

Dolphin Sam Brand is a pseudonym for me, author of "Dolphins Don't Run Marathons."

23798977R00117

Made in the USA
Middletown, DE
04 September 2015